IT'S TIME TO EAT BREAKFAST BURRITOS

It's Time to Eat BREAKFAST BURRITOS

Walter the Educator

Silent King Books
A WhichHead Entertainment Imprint

Copyright © 2024 by Walter the Educator

All rights reserved. No part of this book may be reproduced in any manner whatsoever without written per- mission except in the case of brief quotations embodied in critical articles and reviews.

First Printing, 2024

Disclaimer

This book is a literary work; the story is not about specific persons, locations, situations, and/or circumstances unless mentioned in a historical context. Any resemblance to real persons, locations, situations, and/or circumstances is coincidental. This book is for entertainment and informational purposes only. The author and publisher offer this information without warranties expressed or implied. No matter the grounds, neither the author nor the publisher will be accountable for any losses, injuries, or other damages caused by the reader's use of this book. The use of this book acknowledges an understanding and acceptance of this disclaimer.

It's Time to Eat BREAKFAST BURRITOS is a collectible early learning book by Walter the Educator suitable for all ages belonging to Walter the Educator's Time to Eat Book Series. Collect more books at WaltertheEducator.com

USE THE EXTRA SPACE TO TAKE NOTES AND DOCUMENT YOUR MEMORIES

BREAKFAST BURRITOS

Wake up, wake up, it's a brand-new day,

It's Time to Eat
Breakfast Burritos

Time for breakfast, hip hooray!

The smell so yummy fills the air,

Breakfast burritos, we'll prepare!

A tortilla soft, so warm and round,

Filled with treasures that we've found.

Eggs are scrambled, fluffy and bright,

With cheese that melts, oh, what a sight!

Beans and bacon join the fun,

The perfect way to start the sun.

Some potatoes, crispy and brown,

Inside this wrap, the best around!

Roll it up, nice and neat,

A little bundle, so fun to eat.

Take a bite, it's oh so grand,

The best breakfast in the land!

It's Time to Eat
Breakfast Burritos

A dash of salsa, not too hot,

Adds a zing, a tasty shot!

Maybe avocado, creamy and green,

Breakfast burritos are a dream!

One for you and one for me,

We'll eat together, happy as can be.

Every bite's a burst of cheer,

A breakfast treat that's full of gear!

No forks or spoons, no plates to bring,

Just pick it up, it's the perfect thing!

A meal so easy, wrapped up tight,

Breakfast burritos start the day right.

As we munch, let's smile wide,

With friends and family by our side.

It's Time to Eat
Breakfast Burritos

This morning feast, so fun and yummy,

Fills our hearts and fills our tummy!

When the last bite's gone, we'll say,

"Breakfast burritos saved the day!"

So let's all cheer and clap our hands,

For breakfast burritos, the best in the land!

Tomorrow morning, we'll meet again,

To wrap and roll with our breakfast friends.

Breakfast burritos, hooray, hooray,

It's Time to Eat
Breakfast Burritos

The perfect start to every day!

ABOUT THE CREATOR

Walter the Educator is one of the pseudonyms for Walter Anderson. Formally educated in Chemistry, Business, and Education, he is an educator, an author, a diverse entrepreneur, and he is the son of a disabled war veteran. "Walter the Educator" shares his time between educating and creating. He holds interests and owns several creative projects that entertain, enlighten, enhance, and educate, hoping to inspire and motivate you. Follow, find new works, and stay up to date with Walter the Educator™

at WaltertheEducator.com

www.ingramcontent.com/pod-product-compliance
Lightning Source LLC
LaVergne TN
LVHW052011060526
838201LV00059B/3963